MongoI

IOO16716

Master MongoDB With Simple Steps and Clear Instructions
Second Edition, Revised and Enlarged

By Daniel Perkins

Book Description

This book is a discussion of the functionalities of MongoDB, which is one of the leading NoSQL databases. The first part of the book is an introduction for the user, and especially beginners. They are guided on the basic features of MongoDB.

The process of creating databases and collections in MongoDB has been discussed in this part. You will also learn how to insert, update, and delete data in collections. The vocabularies that are commonly used in MongoDB have also been discussed under this section. You are also guided on how to perform the basic write operations at the various levels of safety and speed.

The process of creating complex queries in MongoDB has been discussed. The book guides you on how to create an application making use of MongoDB and Java programming language. Map Reduce, sharding, aggregation, back up, and restoration processes have been discussed.

Table of Contents

Disclaimer

While all attempts have been made to verify the information provided in this book, the author does assume any responsibility for errors, omissions, or contrary interpretations of the subject matter contained within. The information provided in this book is for educational and entertainment purposes only. The reader is responsible for his or her own actions and the author does not accept any responsibilities for any liabilities or damages, real or perceived, resulting from the use of this information.

The trademarks that are used are without any consent, and the publication of the trademark is without permission or backing by the trademark owner. All trademarks and brands within this book are for clarifying purposes only and are owned by the owners themselves, not affiliated with this document.

Introduction

MongoDB is a powerful database. It is a NoSQL database. It relies on the traditional relational database management system. Databases created in MongoDB offer great scalability, and the performance of these databases is always high. This is why the database is liked by most people. MongoDB offers its users a wide variety of features that they can make use of to manage their databases with little to no difficulty. These databases can also be integrated with software applications developed in various programming languages. This calls for the need for software developers to know how to use MongoDB. This book is an excellent guide for you to learn MongoDB.

Chapter 1 - Get started with MongoDB core concepts and vocabulary

MongoDB is a NoSQL database written in C++. The database is supported on a variety of platforms. The database is document-oriented and relies on a traditional relational-database system. Since it relies on JSON-like documents, integration of this database in certain applications becomes much easy and faster. Since its official release in 2007, the database has become the most common database for use in document stores. It is also number 4 in terms of popularity of database management systems.

Before getting into our practical work, it is important for you to understand some of the vocabulary used in MongoDB.

These are discussed below:

- Database- this is a container that holds the collections. Each database is associated with its own set of database files on the database system. A single MongoDB server usually hosts several databases.

- Collection- these are MongoDB documents grouped together. A particular collection only exists in a particular database. The documents contained in a collection can have several and different fields. The documents that are contained in a particular collection are either similar or related in a way. Collections cannot be used for enforcing a schema.

- Document- this is used to represent a set of key-value pairs. They have a dynamic schema. This indicates that the documents that are contained in a particular collection are not required to have the same collection or be of the same structure. If the fields are the same, then these might be holding different data. Consider the example given below, which is a sample document in MongoDB:

```
{
  _id: ObjectId(6cf79bd7602d)
  title: ' Discussing MongoDB',
  description: 'It is a leading no sql database',
  by: 'John Joel',
  url: 'http://www.mysite.com',
  tags: ['mongodb', 'database', 'NoSQL'],
  likes: 200,
```

```
comments: [
  {
    user:'user1',
    message: 'My comment',
    dateCreated: new Date(2015,12,6,2,20),
    like: 0
  },
  {
    user:'user2',
    message: 'Second comment',
    dateCreated: new Date(2015,12,6,8,47),
    like: 10
  }
 ]
}
```

As you might have noticed, a document should have necessary details such as the id and the title. The user who creates the document owns it. In the above case, John Joel owns the document. The other users, that is, "user1" and "user2" have inserted some data into the document.

Creating a Database

In MongoDB, the following command is used for creation of a database:

use DATABASE_NAME

We have used the command "use" followed by the name of the database, causing a database with that name to be created.

If the specified database name is not in existence, then a new database with that name will be created. If a database with that name is found, then it will be returned. Suppose you want to create a database with the name *"mydatabase"*. You will execute the command *"use mydatabase"* as shown below:

```
> use mydatabase
switched to db mydatabase
>
```

If you want to learn which database is currently selected, use the command *"db"* as shown below:

From the above output, you can see that the user is currently using the database named "mydatabase".

Sometimes, you might need to view the list of available databases in your system. This can be done by use of the command *"show dbs"* as shown below:

```
> show dbs
local    0.078125GB
>
```

From the above output, it is very clear that we only have one database, that is, the "Local" database, in our system. The number on the right side specifies the total size of the database in gigabytes.

Note that although we have created the database *"mydatabase"* in our previous steps, it is not part of the list. For a database to be displayed, insert at least one document into it.

The insertion into our database can be done as shown below:

```
> db.mydatabase.insert({"name":"mysite"})
>
```

We have used the "insert" command for insertion of data into the database. The data is to be inserted into the database named "mydatabase", and in a column "name".

After execution of the above command shows the list of the available databases as shown below:

```
> show dbs
local     0.078125GB
mydatabase          0.203125GB
>
```

The above output shows that the database "mydatabase" was created successfully.

The database "*test*" forms the default database in MongoDB. If you do not create a new database in MongoDB, the collections that you create will be stored in this default database.

Once you have created the database, you might need to drop it. This is done using the command "*dropDatabase()*". This command takes the following syntax:

db.dropDatabase()

Note that the command should be executed with much care so that you don't delete the wrong database. The command executes on the database that is currently in use.

Suppose we need to delete a database named "mydatabase". First we should select the database using the "use" command. This is shown below:

use.mydatabase

The above command will get us into the database "mydatabase", and we can then go ahead to delete it. This can be done by executing the following command:

db.dropDatabase()

You can check for the available database so as to be sure that the deletion was successful. This can be done with the following command:

show dbs

If you execute the above command, the database you have selected will be deleted. If no database has been selected, the default database, which is the "*test*" database, will be deleted. After you execute the command for deletion of the database, check to see whether the database can be found. If you don't find it, it was deleted.

Creating a Collection

For us to create a collection in MongoDB, we use the command "*db.createCollection(name, options)*". The command takes the syntax given below:

db.createCollection(name, options)

The parameter "*name*" is used to specify the name of the collection that is to be created. The parameter "*options*" is used to specify the configuration for the collection. However, this parameter is optional, and there are a number of options that can be used on its behalf. These include the following:

1. **Capped**- this is of type Boolean. When it is set to "*true*", it will enable a capped collection. This is a type of collection with a fixed size. It overwrites the old entries once it has reached the maximum size. If set to "*true*" the size parameter also has to be set.

2. **autoIndexID**- this is also of type Boolean. When it is set to true, it will create an index in the _id field.s. It has a default value of "*false*".

3. **Size**- this parameter is of type number. It is used to specify the maximum size that a capped collection can take. If the parameter "*capped*" is set to "*true*" then you have to specify this parameter.

4. **Max**- this is a parameter of type number. It is used to specify the maximum number of documents that can be accommodated in a capped collection.

While inserting a document, MongoDB will first check the size of the field for the capped collection, then the max field will be checked. The method "*createCollection()*" when used with no parameters is used as follows:

```
> use mydatabase
switched to db mydatabase
> db.createCollection("collection")
{ "ok" : 1 }
>
```

In the above example, we have created a collection named "collection". We have not specified any additional options during the creation of the collection. Note that we have selected the database named "mydatabase" so as to create the collection in the database. Since we see the response "ok" after execution of the command, we know the collection was created successfully.

We have created a collection with the name *"collection"*. To verify the creation of the collection was successful use the command *"show collections"* as shown below:

```
> show collections
collection
```

The above figure shows that our collection creation was a success.

The method *"createCollection()"* can be used together with some extra options. These are shown below:

>db.createCollection("mycollection", { capped : true, autoIndexID : true, size : 6142800, max : 10000 })

In the above case, we have created a collection named "mycollection". Note that the attribute "capped" has been set to true, meaning that the collection will be capped. It will have a fixed size and if we try to exceed that size, then the old entries will be overwritten so as to avoid that. The "autoIndexID" property has also been set to true, meaning that an index will be created for the collection. The maximum size of the collection has been set to 6,142,800, and it will accommodate a maximum of 10,000 documents.

However, for MongoDB users, there is no need to create collections, because they have been created for you. This is done during the time of insertion of a document.

For us to drop a collection from the database, we use the "drop()" method. The method takes the basic syntax given below:

db.COLLECTION_NAME.drop()

To demonstrate how this can be done, begin by checking for the available collections in your database using the "show collections" command. This is shown below:

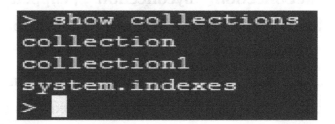

You can then drop any of the collections as shown below:

db.collection1.drop()

This is shown below:

True indicates that the collection has been deleted. You can then check for the available collections in your system to ensure that the deletion ran successfully. This is shown below:

```
> show collections
collection
system.indexes
>
```

The above figure shows that the collection "*collection1*" was deleted from our database, and it is no longer available. If the method has failed, then the result would have been "*false*".

Insertion of Data

In MongoDB, there are two ways you can add data to a collection. These include the use of either the *"insert()"* or *"save()"* method. The *"insert()"* method takes the syntax given below:

>db.COLLECTION_NAME.insert(document)

The "COLLECTION_NAME" refers to the collection that the document is to be inserted into.

Consider the example given below:

```
>db.mycollection.insert({
  _id: ObjectId(7yu5df7sfh7),
  title: 'About MongoDB',
  description: 'MongoDB is one of the leading nosql database',
  by: 'John Joel',
  url: 'http://www.mysite.com',
  tags: ['mongodb', 'database', 'NoSQL'],
  likes: 200
})
```

In the above code, *"mycollection"* is the name of our collection. If the database fails to find this, then it will create a new one and then insert the details in there. If the *"_id"* parameter for the document is not specified, then the database will assign one by default.

We have also specified the title for the document as well as its description. The user inserting the document into the collection is named "John Joel". As you can see, you should make sure that you use single quotes to enclose the content that is to be inserted into the collection.

When you are in need of inserting more than one documents into a database. They can be passed as an array into the *"insert()"* method. This is shown below:

```
>db.post.insert([
{
title: 'About MongoDB',
description: 'MongoDB is one of the leading
NoSQL databases',

by: 'John Joel ',
url: 'http://www.mysite.com',
tags: ['mongodb', 'database', 'NoSQL'],
likes: 100
```

```
},

{
    title: 'Locate Us ',
    description: ' You can call us or email us at any
time you want',

    by: 'John Joel',
    url: 'http://www.mysite.com',
    tags: ['mongodb', 'database', 'NoSQL'],
    likes: 30,
    comments: [
      {
        user:'first_user',
        message: 'MongoDB is a nice database',
        dateCreated: new Date(2015,12,4,11,08),
        like: 0
      }
    ]
  }
])
```

The document can also be inserted using the method "*db.post.save(document)*". In case the parameter "*_id*" for the document is not specified, the database will create a default one. This method takes the following syntax:

>db.COLLECTION_NAME.save({_id:ObjectId(),NEW_DATA})

The following example shows how this method can be used:

db.collection.save(
  <document>,
  {
    writeConcern: <document>
  }
)

Consider the next example given below:

>db.mycollection.save(
  {
    "_id" : ObjectId(2343548781331bcf76ec9),
"title":"An Overview of MongoDB",

    "by":"Author 1"
  }
)
>db.mycollection.find()
{ "_id" : ObjectId(8973548781365bdf45ec8),
"title":"MongoDB New Topic",

"by":"Author 1"}
{ "_id" : ObjectId(59838746781331adf45eb5),
"title":"NoSQL Overview"}

{ "_id" : ObjectId(59756548781231adf45eb8),
"title":"Discussion on MongoDb"}

>

In the above example, we have replaced the document with the
ID **2343548781331bcf76ec9.**

Chapter 2 - Performing basic write operations at different levels of safety and speed

Write concern is used to describe the guarantee that the MongoDB will provide when reporting on how a write operation has been executed. The level of the guarantee is determined by the strength of your write concern. For updates, inserts, and deletes, which have a weak write concern, the write operations are returned quickly. When the write concerns are strong, once a write operation has been sent, the client will wait for the MongoDB to confirm the operation.

Different applications have special needs and this is why there are different levels of write concern to address these special needs. However, the client will have the opportunity to adjust the level of the write concern to meet their desired needs. This is done to ensure that the write operations that are most important persist successfully. If the operations are less critical, you can adjust the write performance to ensure that the performance is improved.

Atomicity and Transactions

In MongoDB, multi-document atomic-transactions are not supported. However, atomic-operations on a single document are supported. This means that for a document having 50 fields, an operation can either update all of these fields or update none. This will mean the atomicity will have been maintained at the document level.

For you to maintain atomicity, it is recommended that you keep all related information in a single document and in the form of an embedded document. The information contained here should be frequently updated. This is a means to ensure that the updates to be made to a document are atomic. Consider the document given below:

```
{
  "_id":1,
  "product_name": "Samsung Galaxy",
  "category": "mobiles",
  " total_products": 20,
  " available_product": 12,
  "product_bought_by": [
    {
      "customer": "joel",
      "date": "7-Dec-2015"
    },
    {
```

```
  "customer": "mercy",
  "date": "10-Dec-2015"
 }
]
}
```

The field *"product_bought_by"* has been used for embedding information about a customer who buys a product. If a new customer comes to buy a product, the field *"available_product"* will be used for checking whether the product is available or not. If there are some products, then the value of the field will be reduced. At the same time, a new customer will be added to the embedded document in the field *"product_bought_by"* field. The command *"findAndModify"* can be used since it finds and updates the document at a go. This is shown below:

```
>db.products.findAndModify({
  query:{_id:3, available_products:{$gt:0}},
  update:{
    $inc:{ available_products:-1},

$push:{product_bought_by:{customer:"gideon",date
:"10-Dec-2015"}}

 }
```

})

The above two mechanisms are for ensuring that the update of the document is only done when the product is available. This will ensure that the transaction is atomic in nature.

Consider a situation in which the information the customer who purchases the device had been kept separately. In this case, the first query will be used for checking on the availability of the product. The second query will then be used for updating the information about the purchase. Suppose there was only one product available. Between the above two transactions, another customer may come in and purchase the product. This will mean that there will be no product available. Despite this, our second query will update the information about the purchase based on the information from the first query. We will then have sold a product that is not available. The database will then be in an inconsistent state.

Bulk Write Operations

In MongoDB, the clients can perform bulk write operations. When used, these usually affect only a single operation. There are different levels of acknowledgement for bulk write operations. There are new bulk operations that can be used for the purpose of inserting, updating, and deleting documents. In bulk insertion, an array of the documents to be inserted can be passed in an array by use of the method *"db.collection.insert()"*.

The bulk write operations can be classified as either *"ordered"* or *"unordered"*. If the operations are ordered, then they have to be executed serially. In case an error is made during the processing of any of the operations in the list, MongoDB has to return and leaves the execution of the rest of the operations.

If the list of the operations is unordered, then the operations can be done in a parallel manner. If an error is made during the execution of one of the operations, then the execution of the rest of the operations will continue as scheduled.

Processing of an unordered list of write operations is faster than executing a list of ordered operations. This is because in the latter case, each operation has to wait for the predecessor to be executed unlike in the former case.

Bulk.insert()

The method takes the syntax given below:

Bulk.insert(**<DOCUMENT>**)

It is used to add a new insert operation to a list of bulk operations. The parameter passed is "*doc*", which specifies the document that is to be inserted. The size of the document to be passed has to be either equal or less than the specified size.

Consider the example given below, which shows how a bulk write operation can be done in MongoDB:

```
var bulkInsert =
db.items.initializeUnorderedBulkOp();
bulkInsert.insert( { item: "xyz123", defaultQty: 50,
status: "A", points: 50 } );

bulkInsert.insert( { item: "abc123", defaultQty: 100,
status: "A", points: 100 } );

bulkInsert.insert( { item: "pqr123", defaultQty: 1,
status: "P", points: 1 } );

bulkInsert.execute();
```

There it is. In the above case, we have initialized the operations builder *"Bulk()"m* for our collection *"items"*. After that, a series of insert operations has been added to multiple documents.

Chapter 3 - Creating complex queries

In MongoDB, we have the option of creating complex queries that can perform complex operations. We are going to discuss these in this chapter.

Limiting Records

The method *"limit()"* is used to limit records in MongoDB. This method only accepts one argument in the form of a number, and this specifies the number of documents to be displayed.

The method takes the syntax given below:

>db.COLLECTION_NAME.find().limit(NUMBER)

The NUMBER is the number of documents that are to be displayed. The COLLECTION_NAME refers to the name of the collection from which the documents are to be selected.

Consider a collection in my database, which has the data given below:

{ "_id" : ObjectId(6735563463781adf45tf67),
"title":"An Overview of MongoDB "}

{ "_id" : ObjectId(78675468781331adf45gh4),
"title":"A NoSQL Database "}

{ "_id" : ObjectId(7845644348781331adf45hj5),
"title":"By John Joel"}

Let us query the database to display only two documents in the above collection:

>db.collection1.find({},{"title":1,_id:0}).limit(2)

The above query will give us the following output:

{"title":"An Overview of MongoDB "}
{"title":" A NoSQL Database"}

Note that we only have two records in the above output, because it is what we have specified. If we don't specify this, then we get all of the documents that are contained in the collection. That is how the method *"limit()"* in MongoDB can be used.

Also, you may have noticed that the query returns the first two documents in the collection. This shows the search began at the top and once it found two documents, it returned them without searching further.

Skipping

This is another method in MongoDB. It requires a single number argument, which specifies the number of documents to be skipped. This means that the method is used for skipping a number of documents.

It takes the syntax given below:

>db.COLLECTION_NAME.find().limit(NUMBER).ski p(NUMBER)

The COLLECTION_NAME is the name of the collection from which the documents are to be skipped. The limit(NUMBER) specifies the number of documents that are to be skipped. The skip(NUMBER) specifies the document number from which the skipping will begin. Note that only the limit(NUMBER) documents will be skipped.

Suppose in the previous collection, we need to display the second document. This can be done as shown below:

>db.collection1.find({},{"title":1,_id:0}).limit(1).skip(1)
{"title":" A NoSQL Database"}
>

In the above example, the skipping should begin from the first document in the collection. Only 1 document should be skipped as specified in the last parameter. This is why the first document is not part of the output. If the last parameter was a 2, then the we would get the last document in the collection. This is because the skipping would begin in document 1, and 2 documents would be skipped, hence the result would be the last document.

You should note that the method "*skip()*" takes a default argument of 0, which means that no document will be skipped.

Sorting Records

The *"sort()"* method is used to sort documents in MongoDB. This method accepts a document that has a list of fields together with the order for sorting. The sorting order is either ascending or descending. Ascending order is represented by 1 while the descending order is represented by -1. The method takes the syntax given below:

>db.COLLECTION_NAME.find().sort({KEY:1})

A situation in which my collection *"collection1"* has the documents shown below:

**{ "_id" : ObjectId(6735563463781adf45tf67),
"title":"An Overview of MongoDB "}**

**{ "_id" : ObjectId(78675468781331adf45gh4),
"title":"A NoSQL Database "}**

**{ "_id" : ObjectId(7845644348781331adf45hj5),
"title":"By John Joel"}**

We need to use the title to sort the documents in a descending order. The following query can be used for this purpose:

```
>db.collection1.find({},{"title":1,_id:0}).sort({"title":
-1})
{"title":"By John Joel"}
{"title":" An  Overview of MongoDB "}
{"title":" A NoSQL Database"}
>
```

As shown above, the display of the documents has been sorted in a descending order based on the title. The alphabets have been used for sorting the documents, and this explains the source of the above output.

In case one does not specify the preference for the sorting, then the documents are displayed in an ascending order. This means that this is the default sorting preference in MongoDB.

Projection

In MongoDB, *"projection"* is a term used to mean the process of selecting only the data that is needed rather than selecting the whole of the data. Suppose your document has 10 records, and you only need 5 of these, you then select only the 5 documents.

The "find()" method

This method in MongoDB is used for accepting the second optional parameter, which is the list of the parameters that one needs to retrieve. Executing this method without specifying the parameter displays all of your documents. For this to be limited, the parameters 1 or 0 must be specified. When 1 is used, the field is shown while when 0 is used, the field is hidden. The method takes the syntax given below:

>db.COLLECTION_NAME.find({},{KEY:1})

Suppose I have a collection with the following documents:

**{ "_id" : ObjectId(6735563463781adf45tf67),
"title":"An Overview of MongoDB "}**

{ "_id" : ObjectId(78675468781331adf45gh4),
"title":"A NoSQL Database "}

{ "_id" : ObjectId(7845644348781331adf45hj5),
"title":"By John Joel"}

Suppose I want to query the titles of the available documents, the following query can be used:

>db.collection1.find({},{"title":1,_id:0})
{"title":" An Overview of MongoDB "}
{"title":" A NoSQL database "}
{"title":"By JohnJoel"}
>

In the above, we have set the "title" to 1, meaning that it should be shown, while the "_id" has been set to 0, meaning that it should not be shown. This is why the titles are part of the output, but the _id field is not part of the output. This shows that once a field has been to 0, then it is hidden, but when it is set to 1, then is displayed.

After querying for documents in MongoDB, the field "_id" is always displayed. To avoid displaying this, set it to 0 as we have done above.

Chapter 4 - Applications with MongoDB

Like other database systems, whether SQL or NoSQL, we can use MongoDB to connect our app to a database. This means that we can use any programming language to create an app, and then connect the app to a MongoDB database. Examples of such programming languages are Java and PHP. Let us discuss how this can be done in Java programming language.

Before getting to use MongoDB and Java, you have to set up the MongoDB Java Driver, and at the same time set up the Java programming environment. In this book, we will not guide you on how to set up Java as this is out of our scope. However, we will show you how to set up the MongoDB Java Driver.

Begin by downloading the latest release of the driver, which is available online for a free download. The file *"mongo.jar"* has to be included in the classpath.

Connecting to the Database

For this to be done, one has to specify the name of the database in which the connection is to be established. If the database is not found, then MongoDB will automatically create a new one.

The code for establishing a connection to the database should be as follows:

```
import com.mongodb.MongoException;
import com.mongodb.MongoClient;
import com.mongodb.DB;
import com.mongodb.DBCollection;
import com.mongodb.BasicDBObject;
import java.util.Arrays;
import com.mongodb.WriteConcern;
import com.mongodb.DBObject;
import com.mongodb.DBCursor;
import com.mongodb.ServerAddress;

public class MongoDBJavaConnection {

    public static void main( String args[] ) {

        try{

            // connecting to the mongodb server
```

```java
    MongoClient mClient = new MongoClient(
"localhost" , 27017 );


    // connecting to the databases
    DB db = mClient.getDB( "mydatabase" );
    System.out.println("Connection to the database
was successful");

    boolean user = db.authenticate(myUserName,
myPassword);

    System.out.println("Authentication: "+user);

   }catch(Exception ex){
    System.err.println( ex.getClass().getName() + ":
" + ex.getMessage() );


    }
   }
}
```

The object "mClient" has been defined to help in specifying the host in which the database is located. In our case, the database is located in the "localhost". The object "db" has then been defined to specify the name of the database we want to establish the connection to. The object "user" has been defined to allow the user to specify the database credentials, that is, the username and password. If the authentication runs successfully, then the connection to the database will be established. You can compile and run the above program. If the connection was successful, then you will get the message "Connection to the database was successful". The message "*Authentication :true*" will be an indication that the provided username and password are correct. If these are wrong, then the connection will fail.

For those who are not aware of how to compile the program, use the following commands:

$javac MongoDBJavaConnection.java
$java -classpath ".:mongo-2.10.1.jar"
MongoDBJavaConnection

We have used the "javac" compiler to compile our program. Ensure that you specify the same name for the class as you used in your program. In my case, the class was named "MongoDBJavaConnection.java". Ensure that you use the correct name.

For Windows users, the following commands can be used:

```
$javac MongoDBJavaConnection.java
$java -classpath ".;mongo-2.10.1.jar"
MongoDBJavaConnection
```

Creating a Collection

Other than creating a collection on the terminal of the database, this can be done by use of a Java program. To do this, we have to call the MongoDB() method *"createCollection()"* within the program.

The following code can be used for creation of a collection in MongoDB:

```
import com.mongodb.MongoClient;
import com.mongodb.DBObject;
import com.mongodb.WriteConcern;

import java.util.Arrays;
import com.mongodb.DBCursor;
import com.mongodb.BasicDBObject;
import com.mongodb.DB;
import com.mongodb.MongoException;import
com.mongodb.DBCollection;
```

```java
import com.mongodb.ServerAddress;

public class MongoDBJavaConnection {

    public static void main( String args[] ) {

        try{

            // connecting to the mongodb server
            MongoClient mClient = new MongoClient(
"localhost" , 27017 );


            // connecting to the databases
            DB db = mClient.getDB( "mydatabase" );
            System.out.println("Connection to the database
was successfully");


            boolean user = db.authenticate(myUserName,
myPassword);

            System.out.println("Authentication: "+user);

            DBCollection collection =
db.createCollection("collection1");
```

```java
        System.out.println("Collection created
successfully");
    }catch(Exception ex){
        System.err.println( ex.getClass().getName() + ":
" + ex.getMessage() );


    }
  }
}
```

You can then compile the program and run it. You can then check at the database level whether the collection was created or not.

Just like in all the Java programs we have written, we have to begin by importing all the necessary libraries. The collection is to be created in a particular database. This means that we have to establish a connection to that database first. Both the username and password have to be used for us to establish that connection, and that is what we have done. The following line of code has been used to create the collection:

db.createCollection("collection1");

The collection has been named "collection1".

How to select a collection

Sometimes, when programming in Java, you might need to select a particular collection in MongoDB to use it. This can be done by calling the method *"getCollection()"* of MongoDB. The code given below shows how this can be done:

```
import com.mongodb.MongoException;
import com.mongodb.WriteConcern;
import com.mongodb.DBObject;
import com.mongodb.MongoClient;
import com.mongodb.DB;
import com.mongodb.DBCursor;
import java.util.Arrays;
import com.mongodb.DBCollection;
import com.mongodb.BasicDBObject;

import com.mongodb.ServerAddress;

public class MongoDBJavaConnection {

    public static void main( String args[] ) {

        try{

            // connecting to the mongodb server
```

```java
        MongoClient mClient = new MongoClient(
"localhost" , 27017 );

        // connecting to the databases
        DB db = mClient.getDB( "mydatabase" );
        System.out.println("Connection to the database
was successful");

        boolean user = db.authenticate(myUserName,
myPassword);

        System.out.println("Authentication: "+user);

        DBCollection coll =
db.createCollection("mycol");
        System.out.println("Collection created
successfully");

        DBCollection collection =
db.getCollection("collection1");
        System.out.println("Collection collection1 was
selected successfully");

    }catch(Exception ex){
        System.err.println( ex.getClass().getName() + ":
" + ex.getMessage() );
```

```
        }
    }
}
```

You can then compile and execute the above program. The collection will be selected successfully. This has been done in the following line:

DBCollection   collection   = db.getCollection("collection1");

In this case we have selected the collection named "collection1".

Inserting a Document

To insert into MongoDB from Java, we have to call the method "*insert()*". Consider the code given for how this can be done:

import com.mongodb.DBCursor;

import com.mongodb.BasicDBObject;

import com.mongodb.MongoClient;

import com.mongodb.MongoException;

import java.util.Arrays;

import com.mongodb.DB;

import com.mongodb.WriteConcern;

```java
import com.mongodb.DBCollection;
import com.mongodb.DBObject;
import com.mongodb.ServerAddress;

public class MongoDBJavaConnection {

    public static void main( String args[] ) {

        try{

            // connecting to the mongodb server
            MongoClient mClient = new MongoClient(
"localhost" , 27017 );

            // connecting to the databases
            DB db = mClient.getDB( "mydatabase" );
            System.out.println("Connection to the database
was successful");

            boolean user = db.authenticate(myUserName,
myPassword);

            System.out.println("Authentication: "+user);
            DBCollection collection =
db.getCollection("collection1");
```

```java
System.out.println("The collection collection1
was selected successfully");


BasicDBObject document = new
BasicDBObject("title", "MongoDB").

    append("description", "database").
    append("likes", 200).
    append("url",
"http://www.mysite.com/mongodb/").
    append("by", "John Joel");

    coll.insert(document);
    System.out.println("The document was inserted
successfully");

    }catch(Exception ex){
    System.err.println( ex.getClass().getName() + ":
" + ex.getMessage() );

    }
   }
}
```

You can then compile and execute the program. The document will be successfully inserted into the database.

Retrieving the Documents

We use the method *"find()"* to select all the documents of the collection in a MongoDB database. Once this method has been used, a cursor will be used and one can iterate through the cursor. The following code snippet can be used for selecting all the documents of a collection:

```
import java.util.Arrays;
import com.mongodb.DBObject;
import com.mongodb.MongoException;
import com.mongodb.MongoClient;
import com.mongodb.DB;
import com.mongodb.DBCollection;
import com.mongodb.BasicDBObject;
import com.mongodb.WriteConcern;
import com.mongodb.DBCursor;
import com.mongodb.ServerAddress;

public class MongoDBJavaConnection{

    public static void main( String args[] ) {
```

```java
try{

    // To connect to mongodb server
    MongoClient mClient = new MongoClient(
"localhost" , 27017 );


    // connecting to the databases
    DB db = mClient.getDB( "mydatabase" );
    System.out.println("Connection to the database
was successful");


    boolean user = db.authenticate(myUserName,
myPassword);

    System.out.println("Authentication: "+user);

    DBCollection collection =
db.getCollection("collection1");
    System.out.println("The collection collection1
was selected successfully");


    DBCursor cursor = collection.find();
    int j = 1;
```

```
    while (cursor.hasNext()) {
      System.out.println("Inserted Document: "+j);
      System.out.println(cursor.next());
      j++;
    }


   }catch(Exception ex){
      System.err.println( ex.getClass().getName() + ":
" + ex.getMessage() );

    }
  }
}
```

Compilation and execution of the above program will give the following result:

Inserted Document: 1

```
{
  "_id" : ObjectId(6ty78ad548913d),
  "title": "MongoDB",
  "description": "database",
  "likes": 200,
  "url": "http://www.mysite.com/mongodb/",
  "by": "John John"
}
```

The document has been retrieved from the database. We created a cursor named "cursor" in the following line:

DBCursor cursor = collection.find();

A variable named "j" has also been defined, and this should be incremented in intervals of 1. With that, the documents will be selected one by one from the collection, and you get your output.

Updating a Document

This can be done by calling the method _"update()"_ of MongoDB. Consider the code given below, which shows how the first document can be updated:

```java
import com.mongodb.BasicDBObject;
import com.mongodb.MongoClient;
import java.util.Arrays;
import com.mongodb.WriteConcern;
import com.mongodb.DBCollection;
import com.mongodb.MongoException;
import com.mongodb.ServerAddress;
import com.mongodb.DBObject;
import com.mongodb.DB;
import com.mongodb.DBCursor;
public class MongoDBJavaConnection {

    public static void main( String args[] ) {

        try{

            // connecting to the mongodb server
            MongoClient mClient = new MongoClient(
"localhost" , 27017 );

            // connecting to the databases
            DB db = mongoClient.getDB( "mydatabase" );
            System.out.println("Connection to the database
was successful");
```

```java
boolean user = db.authenticate(myUserName,
myPassword);

System.out.println("Authentication: "+user);

DBCollection collection =
db.getCollection("collection1");
System.out.println("The collection collection1
was selected successfully");

DBCursor cursor = collection.find();

while (cursor.hasNext()) {
  DBObject upDocument = cursor.next();
  upDocument.put("likes","100")
  collection.update(upDocument);
}

System.out.println("The document was updated
successfully");

cursor = collection.find();

int j = 1;

while (cursor.hasNext()) {
```

```
        System.out.println("Updated Document: "+j);
        System.out.println(cursor.next());
        j++;
    }


    }catch(Exception ex){

        System.err.println( ex.getClass().getName() + ":
" + ex.getMessage() );


        }
    }
}
```

After compiling and executing the above program, the document will be updated. The number of "likes" in the document contained in collection1 will be set to 100, and the update will be completed.

Deleting a Document

We need to demonstrate how the first document in the collection can be deleted. For this to be done, we have to first select the document by use of the method *"findOne()"*. After that, the *"remove"* method of MongoDB can be used. The following code shows how the first document in the collection can be found:

```
import com.mongodb.MongoException;
import com.mongodb.MongoClient;
import com.mongodb.DB;
import java.util.Arrays;
import com.mongodb.BasicDBObject;
import com.mongodb.WriteConcern;
import com.mongodb.DBObject;
import com.mongodb.DBCollection;
import com.mongodb.DBCursor;
import com.mongodb.ServerAddress;

public class MongoDBJavaConnection {

  public static void main( String args[] ) {

    try{
```

```java
// connecting to the mongodb server
MongoClient mClient = new MongoClient(
"localhost" , 27017 );

// connecting to the databases
DB db = mClient.getDB( "mydatabase" );
System.out.println("Connection to the database
was successful");

boolean user = db.authenticate(myUserName,
myPassword);

System.out.println("Authentication: "+user);

DBCollection collection =
db.getCollection("collection1");
System.out.println("The collection collection was
selected successfully");

DBObject myDoc = collection.findOne();
collection1.remove(myDoc);
DBCursor cursor = collection.find();
int j = 1;

while (cursor.hasNext()) {
System.out.println("Inserted Document: "+j);
```

```
        System.out.println(cursor.next());
        j++;
    }


        System.out.println("The document was deleted
successfully");

    }catch(Exception ex){
        System.err.println( ex.getClass().getName() + ":
" + ex.getMessage() );

    }
  }
}
```

You can then compile and execute the above program. The document should be deleted from your collection. The code finds the document named "myDoc" and it is then deleted from the database. You can check at the database level to be sure.

Chapter 5 - Map Reduce

This is a paradigm for processing data in MongoDB in which large volumes of data are condensed, aggregated results that are more useful. For the purpose of carrying out this operation, MongoDB makes use of the command *"mapReduce"*.

The command takes the syntax given below:

>db.collection.mapReduce(
function() {emit(key,value);}, // the map function
function(key,values) {return reduceFunction}, {
//the reduce function

    out: collection,
    query: document,
    sort: document,
    limit: number
  }
)

The following parameters have been used in the above syntax:

- map- this is a JavaScript function for mapping a value with a key and emitting a key-value pair.

- reduce- this is a JavaScript function for reducing or grouping all the documents with the same key

- out- for specifying the location of our map-reduce query result

- query- for specifying the optional selection criteria that selects documents

- sort- for specifying our optional sort criteria

- limit- for specifying the optional maximum number for documents that are to be returned

Consider the document given below:

```
{
   "post_text": "I really like all the tutorials you have
created",
   "user_name": "mercy",
   "status":"active"
}
```

The above code shows a document stored in a MongoDB collection for storing the posts of a user. We now need to use the *"mapReduce"* command to select all the active documents. These should then be grouped based on the username, and then we will count the number of posts for each user.

The following code will be used:

```
>db.posts.mapReduce(
  function() { emit(this.user_id,1); },

  function(key, values) {return Array.sum(values)}, {
    query:{status:"active"},
    out:"total_posts"
  }
)
```

The "mapReduce" query given above should give us the result given below:

```
{
  "result" : "total_posts",
  "timeMillis" : 10,
  "counts" : {
    "input" : 5,
    "emit" : 5,
```

```
  "reduce" : 2,
  "output" : 2
},
"ok" : 1,
}
```

In the above case, you can see that only 5 documents have been matched. 5 of the documents where then emitted. This means that only 5 documents are active. Finally, the documents with the same keys were grouped together into 2 documents.

The "*find()*" function can be used to observe the result we get from the "mapReduce" query:

>db.posts.mapReduce(
function() { emit(this.user_id,1); },
function(key, values) {return Array.sum(values)}, {
query:{status:"active"},
out:"total_posts"
}

).find()

The above query will then give us the result given below:

```
{ "_id" : "mercy", "value" : 2 }
{ "_id" : "joel", "value" : 2 }
```

The output shows that the user *"mercy"* and *"joel"* have 2 posts each that are in an active state.

That is how the query can be used. However, we have shown how it can be used for creating simple queries. The *"mapReduce"*_command can be used for the purpose of constructing very complex queries in MongoDB. By use of custom JavaScript functions, we are able to the "mapReduce" in a flexible manner.

Chapter 6 – Sharding

Sharding means the process in which data records are stored in multiple machines. It is a mechanism used in MongoDB to achieve the property of data growth. As the data increases in size, the machine may not have enough size to accommodate the size of the data. The machine may also not be able to support the appropriate read and write operations on the data. The process of sharding introduces horizontal scaling to solve this problem. With sharding, more machines are added to support the process of data growth. The machines then find it possible to handle the read and write operations.

The need for sharding

- The local disk has not enough space.
- The mater node receives all the writes in time of replication.
- Vertical scaling is expensive.
- If the active dataset is too big, the memory will not be large enough.
- A single replica set is limited to only 12 records.

In MongoDB, sharding is done by use of three components that include the following:

- Shards- these are used for storing the data. They are also good for ensuring that there is availability and that data consistency is maintained.

- Config Servers- these are used for the purpose of storing the metadata for the clusters. This is the data having the mapping data set for the clusters to the shards. The query router makes use of the metadata for targeting the operations to the specific shards. In a production environment, the shard clusters will have 3 configuration clusters.

- Query routers- query routers are instances of Mongos. They work to interface with client applications and in directing the operations to their respective shards. The query router is also responsible for processing and targeting operations to shards, and then returning the results to the clients. A sharded cluster may have more than one query router for dividing the client request load. A client will only send requests to a single query router. A sharded cluster have more query clusters.

Chapter 7 – Backup

The command *"mongodump"* can be use for the purpose of creating a backup in MongoDB. When the command is used, all of the data is dumped into a server in the dump directory. A number of options are available to limit the amount of data or perform a backup of data contained in a remote server. This command takes the syntax given below:

>mongodump

We need to give an example of how the backup can be done in MongoDB.

Begin by launching your MongoDB server. Our assumption is that this server is running on the localhost and on the port 27017. Launch the command prompt, and then navigate to the bin directory of the instance of your MongoDB. Once you are there, execute the command *"mongodump"*.

>mongodump

The above command will establish a connection with the server running at the host 127.0.0.1, which is the localhost and the port 27017. All the data will then be backed up in the server and in the directory "/bin/dump/".

Restoring Data

To restore data in MongoDB, we use the command *"mongorestore"*. When this command is executed, it will restore all the data from the backup directory. This command takes the syntax given below:

>mongorestore

You just have to execute the command on the terminal and all the data will be restored.

Chapter 8 – Aggregation

Aggregation operations are responsible for processing data and returning computed results. These operations group values obtained from different documents and a variety of different operations can be performed on this data to get a single result. MongoDB aggregation can be compared to the *"group by"* clause and the *"count(*)"* operator in SQL.

To do aggregation in MongoDB, we use the *"aggregate()"* method. The method takes the syntax given below:

>db.COLLECTION_NAME.aggregate(AGGREGATE_O PERATION)

Consider a collection in which you are having the following data:

{

  _id: ObjectId(6g9f8ad8990d)

  title: 'An Overview of MongoDB ',

  description: 'MongoDB is a leading no sql database',

  by_user: 'John Joel',

  url: 'http://www.mysite.com',

  tags: ['mongodb', 'database', 'NoSQL'],

  likes: 200

```
},
{
    _id: ObjectId(3cb78ad6502f)
    title: 'A NoSQL Overview',
    description: 'No sql databases are very fast',
    by_user: 'Richard Rotich',
    url: 'http://www.mysite.com',
    tags: ['mongodb', 'database', 'NoSQL'],
    likes: 20
},
{
    _id: ObjectId(6gf78cb8923e)
    title: 'Author Description',
    description: 'A Computer Scientist Phd',
    by_user: 'Author',
    url: 'http://www.author.com',
    tags: ['author', 'database', 'NoSQL'],
    likes: 700
},
```

Now that we have the list given above, we may need to display the list of tutorials created by a particular user. To do this, we have to use the *"aggregate()"* method as shown below:

```
> db.collection1.aggregate([{$group : {_id : "$by_user", num_tutorial : {$sum : 1}}}])
```

```
{
  "result" : [
    {
      "_id" : "John Joel",
      "num_tutorial" : 2
    },
    {
      "_id" : "Description",
      "num_tutorial" : 1
    }
  ],
  "ok" : 1
}
>
```

In the above example, we have used the "user" field to group the tutorials. Note the use of the "by" clause in the selection. As shown in the output, the user named "Joel has created 2 tutorials.

For SQL, the equivalent query will be as shown below:

"select by_user, count(*) from collection1 group by by_user".

In our example given above, we have used the field *"by_user"* to group our documents, and if the user is found, the previous value for him will be incremented.

A list of aggregation operations can be used. These are shown below:

- $sum- this will sum up the defined value from all the documents in our collection.

- $avg- this will calculate the average of the given values from the documents in the collection.

- $min- this is for getting the maximum of our corresponding values from all documents in the collection.

- $max- this is for getting the maximum of our corresponding values from the documents in our collection.

- $push- this is for inserting the values into an array of the resulting documents.

- $first- this is for getting the first document from our source documents according to our grouping.

- $addToSet- this is for inserting the value to an array in our resulting document, but no duplicates will be created.

- $last- this is for getting the last document from our source documents according to our grouping.

The concept of Pipelining

In Unix, pipelining refers to a concept in which the output from a certain command is used as the input for another command. The sequence can then continue. The aggregation framework of MongoDB also supports this concept. However, a set of stages must be followed and each is taken as a document set, which produces a set of documents or JSON documents.

In aggregation framework, the following are some of the possible stages:

- $project: Used when selecting some specific fields from a particular collection.

- $match: a filtering operation with which the amount of documents given as input to our next stage can be reduced.

- $group: this is responsible for doing the actual aggregation.

- $sort: this is for sorting documents.

- $skip: it makes it possible for us to skip forward in our list of documents for the given amount of documents.

- $limit: this is used for limiting on the amount of documents for us to look at by a given number starting from our current position.

- $unwind: This is used for unwinding a document that uses arrays. When we are using an array, our data is like it is pre-joined and the operation will be undone for this to have individual documents. This will make it possible for us to increase the amount of documents for our next stage.

Chapter 9 – Indexing

Indexes are used for supporting the resolution of queries in a more efficient manner. If it were not for indexes, our MongoDB would have to scan our database documents to identify the ones that match depending on the query we formulate. This is an inefficient scan as much data will have to be processed.

Indexes can be viewed as a kind of data structure that stores data in a format that is easy for them to traverse. The index stores the value for a specific field or fields, and these are ordered based on the value of the field as it has been specified in the index.

The method "ensureIndex()"

This method is used to create an index in MongoDB. It takes the syntax given below:

>db.COLLECTION_NAME.ensureIndex({KEY:1})

The key in the above case is used to represent the name of the field for which an index is to be created, and 1 is used to display it in an ascending order. If the index was to be created in a descending order, then we would have set it to -1. An example is given below:

>db.collection1.ensureIndex({"title":1})
>

In case you are in need of creating indexes for multiple fields, then multiple fields can be passed in the above method.

>db.
collection1.ensureIndex({"title":1,"description":-1})
>

Other options that the method can take are discussed below:

- background- this is of type Boolean. It is used for building our index in the background, so that the process of building the index will not block other activities. Set it to *"true"* for building in the background. It has a default value of *"false"*.

- unique- this is also a of type Boolean. It is used for creating a unique index for the collection to deny insertion of documents where the index key or keys will match a value which exists in the index. This should be set to true to create a unique index. It has a default value of *"false"*.

- name- this is of string type. It represents the name of the index. If not specified, MongoDB will generate an index name from concatenation of the names of your indexed fields and sort order.

- sparse- this is of type Boolean. If set to *"true"*, the index will reference only the documents having the specified field. They make use of little space, but they exhibit a different behavior in different situations. It has a default value of *"false"*.

- expireAfterSeconds- this is of an integer data type. It is used for specifying the value in seconds that will control how long MongoDB will retain your documents in the collection.

- v- this is the index version. The default index version will depend on the version of MongoDB you are running when creating your index.

- language_override- this is of type *"string"*. For text index, this is the language that determines the list of the stop words and the rules of the stemmer and tokenizer. It has a default value of *"English"*.

- weights- this is of *"document"* type. It is a number that ranges from 1 to 99,999 and is used for denoting the significance of your field in relation to other indexed fields in terms of score.

- dropDups- this is used for creating a unique index in fields having no duplicates. MongoDB will index only the first occurrence of the key and remove all the documents from your collection that have subsequent occurrences of the key. Set this to *"true"* if you need to create a unique index. It has a default value of *"false"*.

Advanced Indexing

Consider the collection given below:

```
{
  "address": {
    "city": "Lagos",
    "state": "Nigeria",
    "pincode": "123"
  },
  "tags": [
    "music",
    "cricket",
    "blogs"
  ],
  "name": "John Ochukwu"
}
```

How to Index Array Fields

We may need to search for the user documents depending on his tags. For this to be done, we will have to create an index on the array "*tags*" in our collection.

Creation of an index on an array will in turn create separate index entries for each of the fields. After creating an index on our tags array in this case, separate indexes will have to be created for the values music, cricket, and blogs.

For the index to be created on the tags array, the following command can be used:

>db.users.ensureIndex({"tags":1})

Once the index has been created, the tags field of our collection can be searched as follows:

>db.users.find({tags:"cricket"})

To verify on whether the proper indexing was used, use the command given below:

>db.users.find({ tags:" cricket "}). explain()

The command given above will result in a cursor. This will be confirmation that we have used the correct indexing.

Indexing of Sub-Document Fields

We may want to use the fields *"city"*, *"state"*, and *"pincode"* to search for documents in our database. We should now create indexes for the fields of these sub-documents.

The following code can be used for creating this for all of the three fields of the sub-document:

>db.users.ensureIndex({"address.city":1,"address.sta te":1,"address.pincode":1})

Once the index has been created, we can search for a sub-document by use of the index as shown below:

>db.users.find({"address.city":"Lagos"})

Note that the query expression has to follow the order that the index has followed. The index will then be in a position to support the query given below:

```
>db.users.find({"address.city":"Lagos","address.stat
e":"Nigeria"})
```

The following query will also be supported:

```
>db.users.find({"address.city":"Lagos","address.stat
e":"Nigeria","address.pincode":"123"})
```

Limitations of Indexing

1. Overhead- each index created will occupy some space, and it will create an overhead during creation, updating, and deletion of documents. If you do not use your collection on a regular basis to perform a read operation, it is not recommended for you to use indexes.

2. Use of RAM- You should note that the storage of indexes is done in RAM. This calls for the need for you to determine the size of the indexes that you create. Their total size should not exceed the size of your RAM. In case it happens that the size exceeds, then some of the indexes will be deleted and the performance will be lost.

3. Limitations with queries- indexing can be applied to queries using:

  - Regular expressions or the negation operators such as *"$nin", "$not"* and others
  - Arithmetic operators such as *"$mod"* and others.
  - The *"$where"* clause.

This means that one should check how indexes are used for their queries.

4. Index key limits- in MongoDB, an index will not be created in a case where the value of the index field in existence has exceeded the index key limit. However, this has been introduced latest in MongoDB.

5. Insertion of documents that exceed the Index Key Limit

In MongoDB, a document will not be inserted into an indexed collection if the value of the indexed field of the document does exceed the index key limit.

6. Maximum Ranges- the indexes of a collection should not be more than 64. For the case of a compound index, the indexed fields should not be more than 31.

Conclusion

It can be concluded that MongoDB is one of the leading NoSQL databases in the world. It is liked for its good performance and the level of scalability that it offers. Like other databases, software developers can make use of MongoDB for storage of data for their apps. Different programming languages can be linked with a MongoDB app. Examples of these programming languages include Java and PHP. After the connection has been established, one can perform the various operations which can be done at the database level.

Back up and restoration of data can also be done in MongoDB. The appropriate commands have to be used when this is being done. The backup is always done in the *"bin"* directory of the database. This is also where the restoration of the data will be done from. The command *"mapReduce"* is important in MongoDB. With it, the size of a particular volume of data can be reduced. This helps in saving the available storage space. Property sharding is also important. With this, data that is located in different machines is processed efficiently. This is also a technique to cater for data growth. Of course, as data grows in size, it reaches a point in which a certain machine will not be able to support the data. The relevant read and write operations will run slowly. Sharding helps in solving this problem. In MongoDB, indexing is used for the purpose of making sure that the queries executed by the user run efficiently. However, there are certain limitations to indexing. These have been discussed in this book.

Other Books from Daniel Perkins

ASP.NET MVC 5: Learn ASP.net MTV 5 Programming FAST and EASY! (From Zero to Professional Book 1)

http://www.amazon.com/gp/product/B014FV25T8?*Version*=1&*entries*=0

JAVA 8 PROGRAMMING: Step by Step Java 8 Course
Programming (BECOME AN EXPERT Book 1)

http://www.amazon.com/gp/product/B012BDR7CC?*
Version*=1&*entries*=0

C# Programming: UPDATED FOR .NET FRAMEWORK 4.5
(BECOME AN EXPERT Book 2)

http://www.amazon.com/gp/product/B014H2V8XE?
Version=1&*entries*=0

AngularJS: Master AngularJS with Simple Steps and Instructions (From Zero to Professional Book 2)

http://www.amazon.com/gp/product/B016WFXOI6? *Version*=1&*entries*=0

Bootstrap: Practical Guide with Easy to Follow Steps and Instructions (From Zero to Professional Book 3)

http://www.amazon.com/gp/product/B0193WJNKI? *Version*=1&*entries*=0

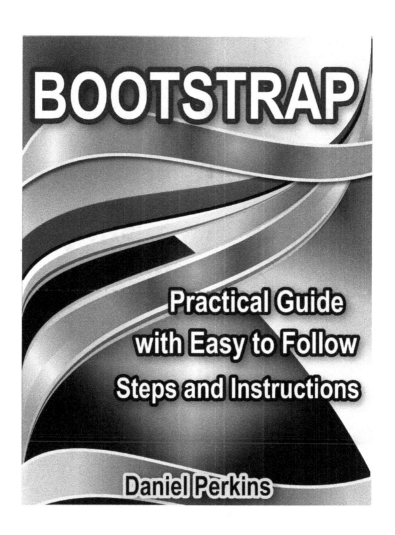

Express.js: Master Express.js and Learn How to Develop Your
Web Application (From Zero to Professional Book 4)

http://www.amazon.com/gp/product/B01B4X2NN8?
Version=1&*entries*=0

MongoDB: Master MongoDB with Simple Steps and Clear
Instructions (From Zero to Professional Book 5)

http://www.amazon.com/gp/product/B01B4X2NU6?
Version=1&*entries*=0